# Celebrate the 50 States!

written and illustrated by **Loreen Leedy**

**Holiday House**

New York

This book is dedicated to the men and women who founded our nation.

## Key to Labels

| | |
|---|---|
| **State rank** | 22nd |
| **Year entered Union** | 1819 |
| **State capital** | *Montgomery* |
| **Town** | *Huntsville* |
| **State bird and flower** | Yellowhammer, Camellia |
| **Other animal** | Opossum |
| **Place or event** | *Tuskegee Institute* |
| **Product from state** | paper pulp |
| **Scale of map** | *60 miles* |
| **Ocean or Lake** | *Gulf of Mexico* |
| **River** | *Chattahoochee River* |

Library of Congress Cataloging-in-Publication Data
 Leedy, Loreen.
Celebrate the 50 states / written and illustrated by Loreen Leedy.
p. cm.
Summary: Introduces statistics, emblems, notable cities, products, and other facts about the fifty states, United States territories, and Washington, D.C.
ISBN 0-8234-1431-0
1. U.S. states Miscellanea Juvenile literature. 2. United States Miscellanea Juvenile literature. [1. United States Miscellanea.]
I. Title.
E180.L44 1999   973—dc21   99-10986   CIP

Reprinted by arrangement with Holiday House.
10  9  8  7  6  5  4  3  2

Thanks to my brother Robert Leedy for his help in finding reference materials.

Here is what you'll find in this book:

| | | | |
|---|---|---|---|
| Alabama, Alabama | 4 | New Hampshire, New Jersey | 18 |
| Arizona, Arkansas | 5 | New Mexico, New York | 19 |
| California, Colorado | 6 | North Carolina, North Dakota | 20 |
| Connecticut, Delaware | 7 | Ohio, Oklahoma | 21 |
| Florida, Georgia | 8 | Oregon, Pennsylvania | 22 |
| Hawaii, Idaho | 9 | Rhode Island, South Carolina | 23 |
| Illinois, Indiana | 10 | South Dakota, Tennessee | 24 |
| Iowa, Kansas | 11 | Texas, Utah | 25 |
| Kentucky, Louisiana | 12 | Vermont, Virginia | 26 |
| Maine, Maryland | 13 | Washington, West Virginia | 27 |
| Massachusetts, Michigan | 14 | Wisconsin, Wyoming | 28 |
| Minnesota, Mississippi | 15 | Washington, D.C. | 29 |
| Missouri, Montana | 16 | U.S. Territories | 29 |
| Nebraska, Nevada | 17 | United States map | 30 – 31 |
| | | Answers | 32 |

# Alabama

Yellowhammer

Alabama is a warm southern state.

**22nd**

*Our rocket was made in Huntsville.*

1969: Apollo 11 lands on moon

1819

Space and Rocket Center

**Huntsville**

Opossum

*Why is Rosa Parks famous?*

*Cotton clothing feels good in hot weather.*

**Birmingham**

Tuskegee Institute

Chattahoochee River

**Montgomery**

60 miles

Gulf of Mexico

Camellia

paper pulp

iron

steel

# Alaska

Alaska is the **largest** and coldest state.

Polar bear

**49th**

North Pole

Prudhoe Bay oil field

1959

Arctic Ocean

Orca

Walrus

Trans-Alaska Pipeline

*How much did Alaska cost?*

GOLD

**Nome**

Musk Ox

Malamute sled dog

Caribou

*Mt. McKinley*

**Anchorage**

200 miles

**Juneau** ★

Willow Ptarmigan

Pacific Ocean

*Mt. McKinley is the highest peak in North America.*

Forget-me-not

*Native people carved totem poles to show their family clan.*

# Arizona

Arizona has a dry climate and unusual scenery, with mesas, canyons, and rock formations.

48th

1912

100 miles

The Grand Canyon

Monument Valley

Petrified Forest National Park

Flagstaff

The Arizona Meteor Crater

Irrigation helps us grow.

The Petrified Forest is full of fossilized trees.

Phoenix

Tucson

OK CORRAL

Cactus Wren

Saguaro Cactus Flower

How deep and how long is the Grand Canyon?

Navajo weavers make beautiful wool rugs.

# Arkansas

Arkansas is called the natural state, because of its mountains, forests, waterfalls, lakes, rivers, and mineral springs.

25th

1836

Fayetteville

Ozark Folk Center

Bobcat

Little Rock

Rice Fields

Hot Springs

Mississippi River

60 miles

Turkey Tidbits

Mockingbird

You may have eaten rice and processed foods from this state.

What precious stones can be dug up in Arkansas?

Apple Blossom

We like to go canoeing on the Buffalo River.

# California

**Redwoods** World's Tallest Trees

More people live in California than in any other state.

31st

1850

California Valley Quail

*Half Dome, Yosemite National Park*

**Sacramento**

Sea Lion

**San Francisco**

computers

I was made in Silicon Valley.

How hot can it get in Death Valley?

Movie stars want to win me.

*Mohave Desert*

*Pacific Ocean*

• Los Angeles    Joshua Tree

100 miles

I like the sunshine and surfing in California, but not the earthquakes!

Our state grows the most fresh produce.

Golden Poppy

# Colorado

People who come to Colorado enjoy skiing and hiking in the Rocky Mountains.

38th

1876

*Dinosaur National Monument*    *Rocky Mountain National Park*

**Boulder•**

What ferocious dinosaurs used to live in Colorado?

**Denver**

I was made at the U.S. Mint in Denver.

•Aspen

*Mesa Verde National Park*

100 miles

These cliff dwellings were built long ago.

Rocky Mountain Columbine

Lark Bunting

Bighorn Sheep

6

Robin

## CONNECTICUT

5th
1788

Connecticut's factories make submarines, clocks, helicopters, hardware, locks, and silverware.

clocks

30 miles

*Hartford*

*Who wrote America's first dictionary?*

Mountain Laurel

Raccoon

YALE

**New Haven**

**Mystic**

Long Island Sound

submarines

*Mystic Seaport is a restored 19th-century waterfront town.*

# Delaware

1st
1787

Delaware was the first of the 13 colonies to become a state.

*What was invented here in 1935?*

**Wilmington**

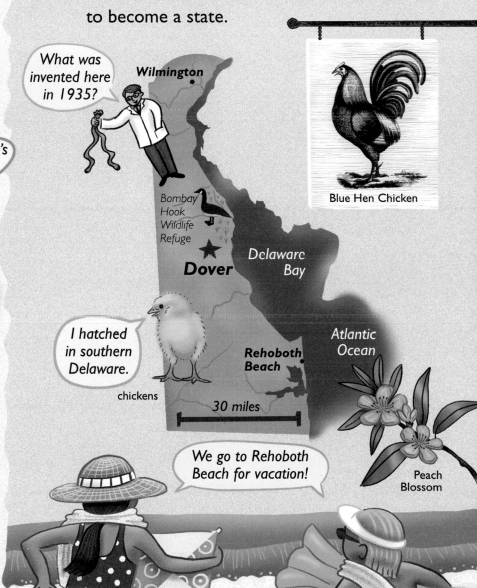

Blue Hen Chicken

*Bombay Hook Wildlife Refuge*

**Dover**

*Delaware Bay*

*I hatched in southern Delaware.*

**Rehoboth Beach**

*Atlantic Ocean*

chickens

30 miles

*We go to Rehoboth Beach for vacation!*

Peach Blossom

# Florida

**27th** 1845

Florida is a flat peninsula with more than a thousand miles of sandy beaches.

What is the largest wetlands on earth?

Mockingbird

Alligator

Gulf of Mexico

★ **Tallahassee**

100 miles

Manatee

grapefruit

*Theme Parks!*

**Orlando** •

Orange Blossom

honey

Atlantic Ocean

Kennedy Space Center

**Miami**

The Everglades

*Florida Keys*

Bottle-nosed dolphin

# GEORGIA

**4th** 1788

Georgia is the largest state east of the Mississippi River.

One end of the Appalachian Trail is in Georgia. How far does it go?

Cherokee Rose

watermelon

peanuts

peaches

Stone Mountain

★ **Atlanta**

pecans

*Grown in Georgia*

Brown Thrasher

*Masters Golf Tournament*

**Augusta**

80 miles

**Savannah** •

Cypress Tree

*Okefenokee Swamp*

Atlantic Ocean

Civil rights leader Martin Luther King, Jr., was born in Atlanta.

**8**

# HAWAII

**50th** 1959

The nation's youngest state is a chain of islands. Each island is the top of an underwater mountain.

World's most rain: 460 inches a year

Mt. Waialeale

Niihau
Kauai
Pacific Ocean

Oahu
**Honolulu**
Pearl Harbor

Molokai
**Wailuku**
Lanai
Maui
Kahoolawe
80 miles

Hawaii

Hilo
Mauna Loa volcano

pineapple

*Product of Hawaii*

*Surfing was invented by Hawaiians.*

Nene

*Aloha! How many letters does the Hawaiian language have?*

*The hula is a traditional dance. It is often performed at a luau (a big feast).*

Diamond Head (extinct volcano)

Yellow Hibiscus

# Idaho

**43rd** 1890

potatoes          silver

Idaho has many mountains and miles of rivers.

*What causes whitewater in a river?*

1805 Lewis & Clark camped here

Lewiston

100 miles

*whitewater rafting*

Sun Valley

**Boise**

*We grow the most potatoes!*

Mountain Bluebird

Snake River

**Twin Falls**

Sawtooth Range

Cougar

Syringa

9

# ILLINOIS

**21st**
**1818**

railroad cars

**19th**
**1816**
Indiana

Illinois has quiet farms in the countryside and busy urban areas. Chicago is a great city that is a hub for shipping by land, air, and water.

*How many stories does the Sears Tower have?*

Like other Midwestern states, Indiana has cornfields, small towns, cold winters, and hot summers.

Illinois Violet

Lake Michigan

Chicago

Peoria

**Springfield**

soybeans

80 miles

Lake Michigan

Gary

Peony

80 miles

Ft. Wayne

Children's Museum

Basketball is very popular in Indiana.

"Indy 500" Motor Speedway

**Indianapolis**

Cardinal

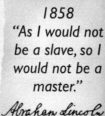

Cardinal

1858
"As I would not be a slave, so I would not be a master."
*Abraham Lincoln*

Lincoln Boyhood National Memorial

The nation's oldest zoo has free admission.

Lincoln Park Zoo, Chicago

Abraham Lincoln lived in both Illinois and Indiana. He became one of the country's most beloved presidents.

*What is a Hoosier?*

# Iowa

hogs

29th
1846

Iowa has over 100,000 farms. The biggest crops are corn and soybeans.

Who painted us?

80 miles

This state has great topsoil!

• Sioux City

Des Moines

• Cedar Rapids

Mississippi River

National Balloon Museum

Wild Rose

My calf won a prize at the Iowa State Fair.

Eastern Goldfinch

CORNDOGS

# Kansas

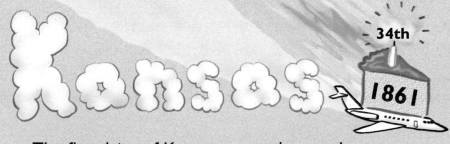

34th
1861

The flat plains of Kansas grow wheat and other "amber waves of grain." Many private airplanes and small jets are made in Wichita.

Geographic Center of the Lower 48 states

Topeka

Why did cowboys come to Dodge City in the 1880s?

World's Largest Salt Deposit

National Teachers Hall of Fame

• Dodge City          • Wichita

100 miles

1932
First Woman to Fly Atlantic Solo
Amelia Earhart was born in Kansas.

helium

Sunflower

Western Meadowlark

Flour

Some foods made of wheat

# Kentucky

The Bluegrass State was nicknamed for its blue-green grass.

15th
1792

Kentucky Derby

Kentucky Cardinal

100 miles

Goldenrod

Louisville

**Frankfort**

Ohio River

Horse Farms

Mammoth Cave

Grass Seed

**Bowling Green**

Whose gold is stored in Fort Knox?

Mammoth Cave is the largest cave system in the world. It has over 300 miles of passages.

# LOUISIANA

18th
1812

The Mississippi River makes New Orleans one of the busiest ports in America.

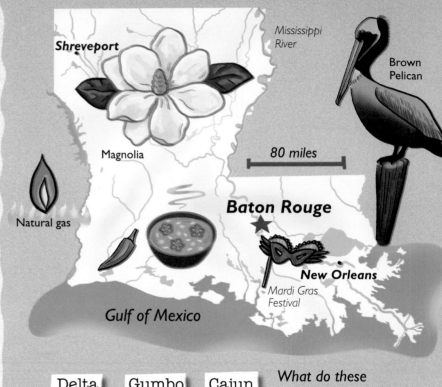

**Shreveport**

Mississippi River

Magnolia

Brown Pelican

Natural gas

80 miles

**Baton Rouge**

**New Orleans**

Mardi Gras Festival

Gulf of Mexico

Delta   Gumbo   Cajun

What do these Louisiana words mean?

Jazz began in New Orleans.

# MAINE

**23rd**
**1820**

Maine has many lighthouses to warn boats away from its rocky coast.

Christmas trees

Maine Coon Cat

*Look, it's a whale!*

lobster

60 miles

toothpicks

sardines

**Bangor**

**Augusta** ★

**Portland**

Atlantic Ocean

Who sees the sun rise earliest in the fifty states?

Chickadee

White Pine Cone and Tassel

Moose

# Maryland

**7th**
**1788**

crabs

oysters

Maryland has a very long shoreline, with plenty of seafood to catch and eat.

Chesapeake Bay Retriever

*National Aquarium*

Black-eyed Susan

60 miles

**Baltimore**
**Annapolis**

*Washington, D.C. Capital of U.S.A.*

**Salisbury**

Chesapeake Bay

*"Oh say, can you see, by the dawn's early light..."*

*What song is that?*

Baltimore Oriole

# Massachusetts

6th
**1788**

Many historic events took place in Massachusetts.

Chickadee

1620
Pilgrims land

1621
The First Thanksgiving

1773
The Boston Tea Party

1775
Paul Revere's ride

Cranberries

1636
1st U.S. College
Harvard

SALEM

Worcester •

**Boston**

Atlantic Ocean

Plymouth •

Cape Cod

Mayflower

Cape Cod

40 miles

What was the name of the Pilgrims' ship?

Codfish

# Michigan

26th
**1837**

Michigan is made of two peninsulas surrounded by four of the Great Lakes.

Apple Blossom

100 miles

Lake Superior

snowmobiling

Mackinac Bridge

Robin

Whitetail Deer

Sleeping Bear Dunes National Lakeshore

Lake Huron

Lake Michigan

**Grand Rapids**

**Lansing**

**Detroit** •

Flakies!

cereal

Lake Erie

What is the nickname for the Lower Peninsula?

Detroit is known as the Motor City because so many cars and trucks are made there.

# Minnesota

St. Paul
Winter Carnival

32nd

1858

Minnesota has cold winter weather and many lakes and forests.

100 miles

Gopher

Luke Itasca, the source of the Mississippi River

Mississippi River

Duluth

Showy Lady Slipper

Minneapolis.

St. Paul

St. Paul and Minneapolis are very close together. They are known as the Twin Cities.

The thousands of lakes in this state are the footprints of my big blue ox, Babe!

I don't think so. Who are you, anyway?

Loon

**15**

# Mississippi

20th

1817

Mississippi has the look of the Old South, with many pre-Civil War houses still standing.

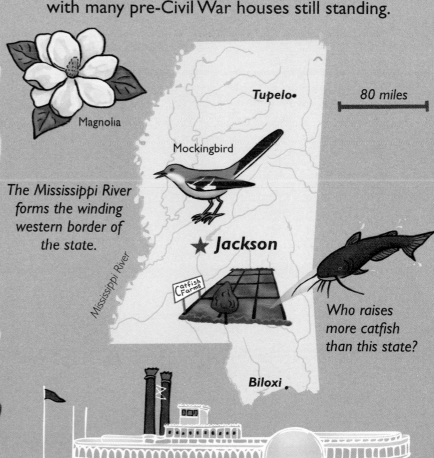

Magnolia

Tupelo•

80 miles

Mockingbird

The Mississippi River forms the winding western border of the state.

Mississippi River

★ Jackson

Catfish Farms

Who raises more catfish than this state?

Biloxi.

Paddle Steamboat

# Missouri

1821

Missouri was the "Gateway to the West" when many pioneers traveled through.

*For how long did the Pony Express deliver mail?*

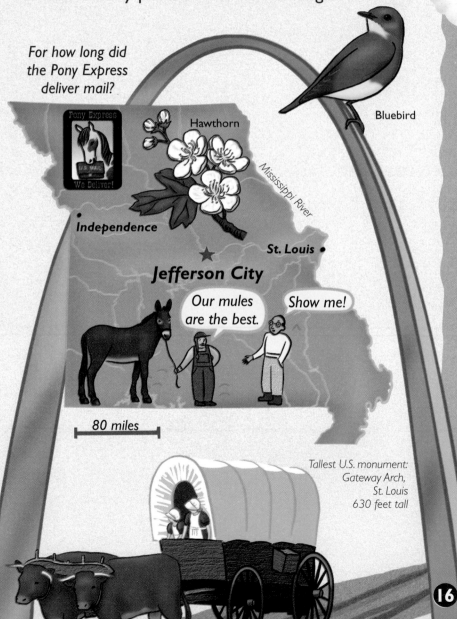

Pony Express
We Deliver!

Hawthorn

Mississippi River

Independence

St. Louis

★ Jefferson City

*Our mules are the best.*

*Show me!*

Bluebird

80 miles

Tallest U.S. monument:
Gateway Arch,
St. Louis
630 feet tall

# Montana

41st

1889

Montana has wide open spaces with fewer than a million residents.

*"Big Sky Country" is the state's nickname.*

Western Meadowlark

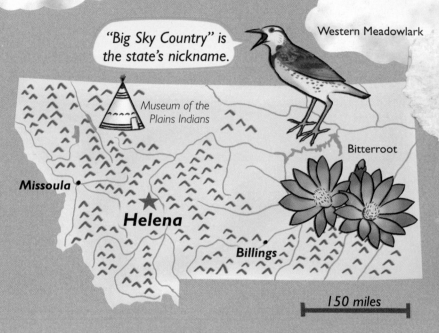

Museum of the Plains Indians

Bitterroot

Missoula

**Helena**

Billings

150 miles

*What are glaciers made of?*

Glacier National Park

Mountain Goat

# Nebraska

**37th**

**1867**

Western Meadowlark

Most of Nebraska's land is used for farming.

Goldenrod

*What holiday was started in this state?*

Missouri River

Chimney Rock

corn
cattle
wheat

North Platte

Omaha •

**Lincoln** ★

100 miles

Mammoth

*I wish mammoths still lived in Nebraska!*

# NEVADA

Mountain Bluebird

Nevada has the lowest rainfall of any state.

**36th**

**1864**

*What is its average rainfall every year?*

Lake Tahoe

Rattlesnake

*Much of Nevada is desert.*

Reno
•

★ **Carson City**

Sagebrush

120 miles

*Gambling is legal in Nevada.*

Las Vegas

Hoover Dam

*Bristlecone pines are the oldest living things in the world.*

# New Hampshire

New Hampshire's colorful fall leaves, crisp winters, and quiet villages are typical of New England states.

*That covered bridge is really long.*

*Why do they cover bridges, anyway?*

40 miles

Purple Lilac

1934
World's fastest wind speed was recorded on Mt. Washington: 231 miles per hour!

Concord

Purple Finch

• Manchester

Nashua •

This state holds the first primary for every presidential election.

VOTE

*I am the Old Man of the Mountain.*

# New Jersey

New Jersey is densely populated and has many farms and beaches.

Boardwalk Boogie

Eastern Goldfinch

30 miles

Newark •

*Who invented the light bulb in his lab in New Jersey?*

Trenton

Atlantic Ocean

Grown in the Garden State

Cape May has many Victorian-style buildings.

Atlantic City •

Cape May

Purple Violet

18

# New Mexico

Old traditions as well as modern technology are a part of life in New Mexico.

**47th**

**1912**

People can build with adobe in a dry climate.

What is adobe?

Pueblo village

**Santa Fe**

I am a storyteller doll.

• **Albuquerque**

1945
The first atomic bomb tested

**Las Cruces.**

Carlsbad Caverns

100 miles

Bat

Yucca

Pueblo pottery

Roadrunner

White Sands National Monument

**19**

# NEW YORK

**11th**

**1788**

Nature lovers enjoy visiting New York state's mountains and lake shorelines.

Bluebird

100 miles

*Lake Ontario*

Niagara Falls

The Finger Lakes are long and thin... like fingers!

**• Buffalo**

**Albany**

New York City is the nation's largest city, with endless things to see and do.

Long Island

theater

art

**New York City**

finance

shopping

fashion

Statue of Liberty

New York City skyline

Rose

What country gave me to the United States?

# North Carolina

12th

1789

North Carolina has mountains in the west, hills in the center, and beaches in the east.

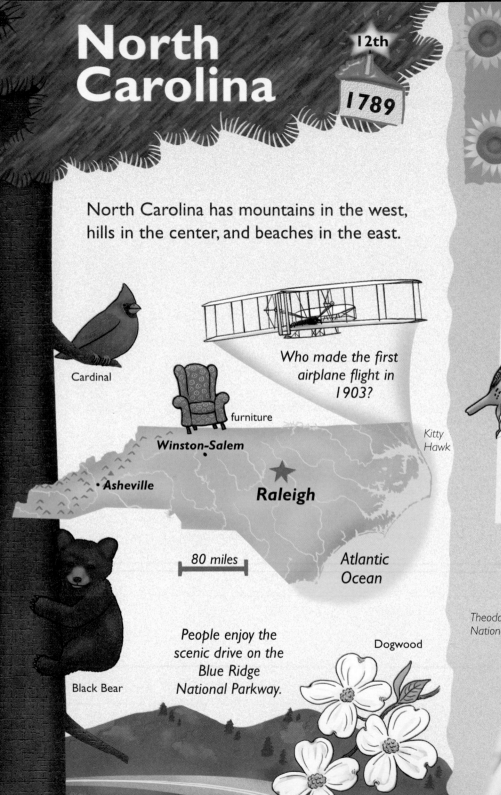

Cardinal

*Who made the first airplane flight in 1903?*

furniture

Winston-Salem

Kitty Hawk

• Asheville

★ **Raleigh**

80 miles

*Atlantic Ocean*

Black Bear

*People enjoy the scenic drive on the Blue Ridge National Parkway.*

Dogwood

# North Dakota

39th

1889

Homesteaders came to North Dakota in the late 1800s to farm.

WHEAT

*International Peace Garden*

*What is a homesteader?*

Western Meadowlark

Wild Prairie Rose

**Grand Forks**

Fargo •

★ **Bismarck**

Pronghorn

100 miles

Theodore Roosevelt National Park

*Sitting Bull was a leader of the Sioux Nation.*

# Ohio

Ohio has many factories that produce rubber, office machines, refrigerators, glass, and more.

Cardinal

Scarlet Carnation

How many U.S. presidents were born in Ohio?

Lake Erie

• **Cleveland**

Rock and Roll Hall of Fame

Amish buggy

**Columbus**

**Cincinnati** • Serpent Mound

Ohio River

80 miles

The arts and sciences are important in Ohio.

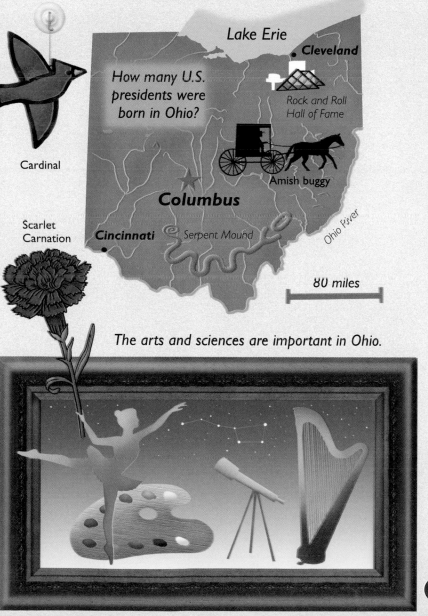

21

# Oklahoma

Oklahoma is home to more American Indians than any other state.

There's an oil well in front of the state capitol building!

100 miles

• Tulsa

★ **Oklahoma City**

• **Lawton**

Rose rocks are natural crystal formations.

What were "sooners"?

Scissor-tailed Flycatcher

Mistletoe

Everything is funny as long as it's happening to somebody else.

Cowboy humorist Will Rogers 1879–1935

# Oregon

lumber

Western Meadowlark

Immigration to this state began in 1842 along the Oregon Trail.

33rd

**1859**

100 miles

Gray whale

Portland

Mt. Hood

Salem

Bend

*I thought we'd never get here!*

Pacific Ocean

Peppermint Oil

Oregon Grape

*Salmon fishing is a big industry in Oregon.*

Crater Lake

How deep is Crater Lake?

**22**

# Pennsylvania

Ruffed Grouse

In 1776, the Continental Congress signed the Declaration of Independence in Philadelphia.

2nd

**1787**

60 miles

coal

Mountain Laurel

steel

The Liberty Bell

**Harrisburg**

Pittsburgh

*Philadelphia*

*Pennsylvania had the nation's first:*

library

hospital

art museum

fire department

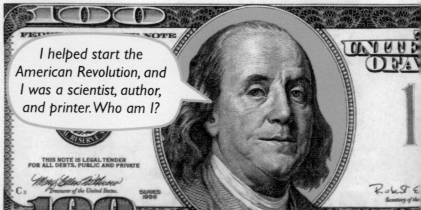

*I helped start the American Revolution, and I was a scientist, author, and printer. Who am I?*

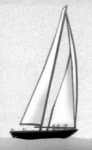

# Rhode Island

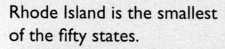
13th
1790

*America's Cup Yacht Race*

Rhode Island is the smallest of the fifty states.

Violet

*Is Rhode Island really an island?*

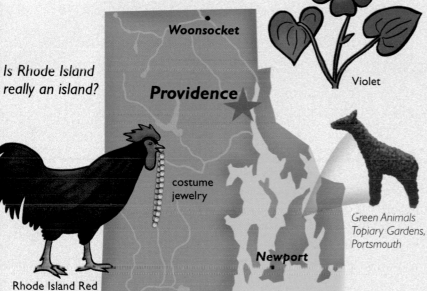

**Providence**

**Woonsocket**

costume jewelry

Green Animals Topiary Gardens, Portsmouth

**Newport**

Rhode Island Red

20 miles

Atlantic Ocean

Rhode Island has many mansions that overlook the ocean.

The Breakers, Newport

**23**

# South Carolina

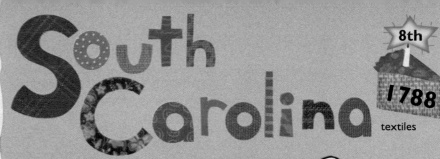
8th
1788
textiles

South Carolina has hot, humid summers and mild winters.

Yellow jessamine

• Greenville

**Columbia**

Carolina Wren

peaches

sweetgrass basket

**Charleston** •

80 miles

*Where did the Civil War begin?*

Atlantic Ocean

Magnolia Gardens, Charleston

Hilton Head lighthouse

# South Dakota

Pasqueflower

Most of South Dakota is prairie grasslands.

"Many of my books about pioneer life took place in this state. Who am I?"

Ring-necked Pheasant

Rapid City

**Pierre**

Sioux Falls

*Badlands National Park*

80 miles

ring made of Black Hills gold

*The giant sculpture of four U.S. presidents on Mt. Rushmore is world famous.*

# Tennessee

*Great Smoky Mountains*

Tennessee is known for mountains and country music.

"Don't be cruel... to a bird so cool..."

"What famous singer had a mansion in Memphis?"

Mockingbird

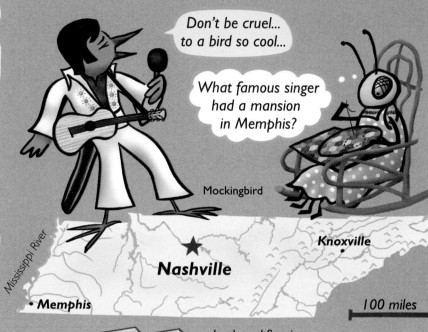

Mississippi River

Knoxville

**Nashville**

• **Memphis**

100 miles

hardwood flooring

Iris

*The steepest passenger railway in the world goes up Lookout Mountain in Chattanooga.*

INCLINE RAILWAY

"We can see for miles from up here!"

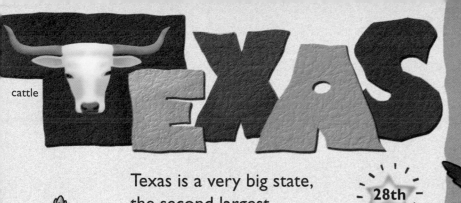
**TEXAS**

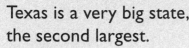
cattle

Texas is a very big state, the second largest.

28th

1845

Just call me Tex.

Bluebonnet

Mockingbird

*Dallas*

Armadillo

McDonald Observatory

**Austin**

*Houston*

mariachi dancers

180 miles

Gulf of Mexico

oil drilling and refining

Why do we "remember the Alamo"?

---

**Utah**

45th

1896

Petroglyphs

Mormon pioneers came to Utah in 1847.

What did seagulls do that helped Utah's settlers to survive?

California Gull

Great Salt Lake

**Ogden**

100 miles

**Salt Lake City**

• **Provo**

copper

snowboarding

Pioneer journal

Bryce Canyon National Park

Arches National Park

Utah's landscape has thousands of fantastic rock formations.

Sego Lily

**25**

# Vermont

Vermont is a rural state with small towns, villages, and farms.

14th
1791

granite

marble

Red Clover

Green Mountains

• Burlington

★ Montpelier

• Rutland

40 miles

Hermit Thrush

How do people make maple syrup?

Biking, hiking, and skiing are popular sports in Vermont.

# Virginia

10th
1788

The first successful English colony was founded in Jamestown, Virginia, in 1607.

Dogwood

Cardinal

Alexandria •

Jamestown artifacts

80 miles

★ Richmond

hams

Norfolk •

Atlantic Ocean

Visitors come to Williamsburg to see how the colonists lived.

Candle making

George Washington is known as the father of our country. Why is Virginia nicknamed "Mother of Presidents"?

# Washington

Willow Goldfinch

42nd
1889

Washington has wet weather in the west and a dry climate in the east.

Sea otter

*We make jets that fly all over the world.*

80 miles

Space Needle, Seattle

Olympic rain forest

•Seattle

apples

Spokane •

cherries

Pacific Ocean

★ **Olympia**

Mt. Rainier

Mt. St. Helens

Coast Rhododendron

*Which mountain erupted in 1980 and sent ashes drifting for hundreds of miles?*

# West Virginia

35th

glass

1863

West Virginia used to be part of Virginia, but became a separate state during the Civil War.

*Our state is very mountainous, with hardly any flat land at all.*

**Wheeling** •

rock climbing

60 miles

Ohio River

*Coal mining is hard work.*

Cardinal

**Huntington**
•

★ *Charleston*

*Why is coal called a fossil fuel?*

Grist Mill, Babcock State Park

Rhododendron

# Wisconsin

Badger

Wisconsin has thousands of lakes that were formed by glaciers a long time ago.

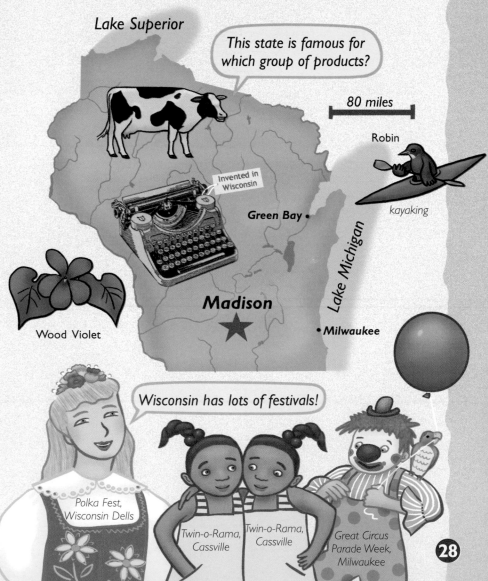

Lake Superior

This state is famous for which group of products?

80 miles

Robin

kayaking

Invented in Wisconsin

Green Bay •

Lake Michigan

Wood Violet

**Madison**

• **Milwaukee**

Wisconsin has lots of festivals!

Polka Fest, Wisconsin Dells

Twin-o-Rama, Cassville

Twin-o-Rama, Cassville

Great Circus Parade Week, Milwaukee

**28**

# Wyoming

Frontier Days, Cheyenne

Wyoming has the smallest population of all the states.

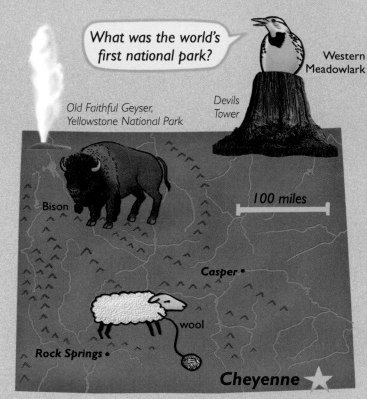

What was the world's first national park?

Western Meadowlark

Old Faithful Geyser, Yellowstone National Park

Devils Tower

**Bison**

100 miles

**Casper** •

wool

**Rock Springs** •

**Cheyenne** ★

Lower Falls, Yellowstone

Indian Paintbrush

Grizzly bear

# Washington, D.C.
## (District of Columbia)

The U.S. government is located in Washington, D.C. Senators and representatives are elected by each state to come here.

*National Zoo*

*The White House*

*That's where the president lives!*

*Which state donated the land where Washington, D.C., now stands?*

*The Mall is lined with government buildings, museums, and monuments.*

|———| 5 miles

*Lincoln Memorial*

*Vietnam Veterans Memorial*

*Washington Monument*

*Potomac River*

*Smithsonian Institution*

*U.S. Capitol*

# U.S. Territories

The largest U.S. territory is the Commonwealth of Puerto Rico.

**Guam**
***Agaña***

*U.S. military bases*

|———| 40 miles

*Guam and American Samoa are small islands in the Pacific.*

*Millions of tourists visit the islands every year.*

**San Juan**

bananas

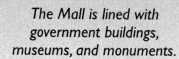

Puerto Rico

• **Mayagüez**

sugar cane

**Ponce** •

*Pacific Ocean*

**Charlotte Amalie**

St. John

St. Thomas

*Atlantic Ocean*

U.S. Virgin Islands

oil refining

St. Croix

**Pago Pago**

American Samoa

*Are the people who live in these territories U.S. citizens?*

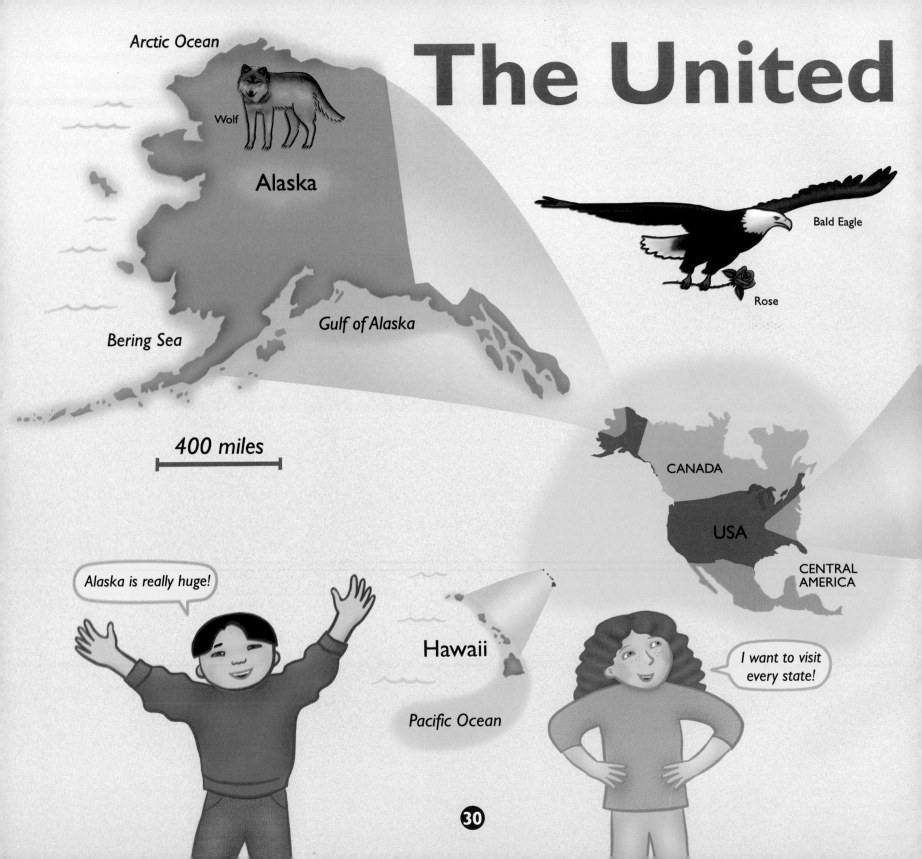

# States of America

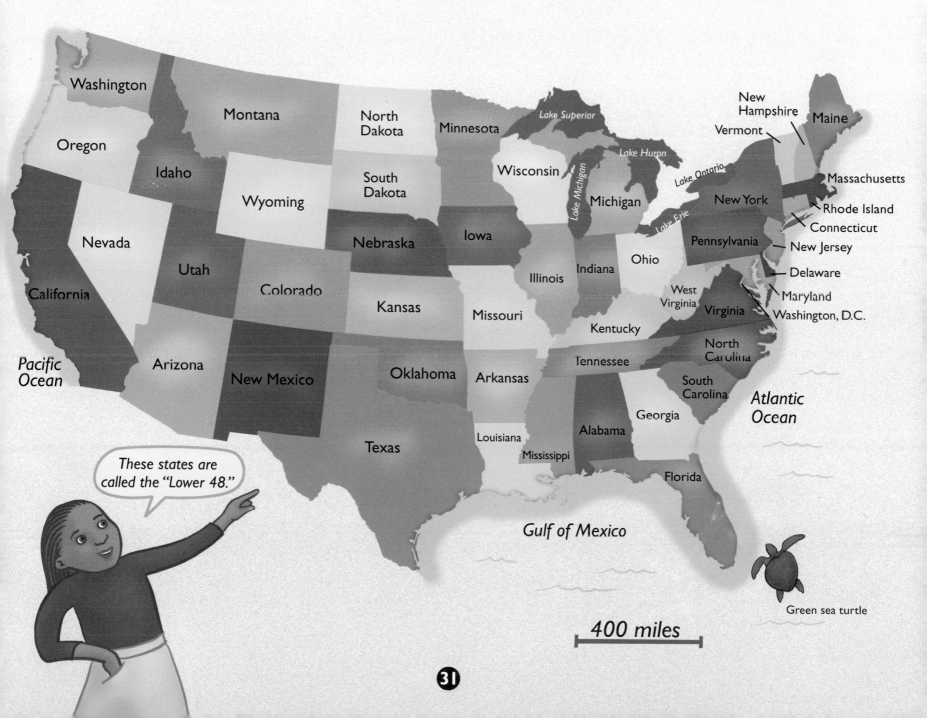

# Answers

page 4 **AL** In 1955, Rosa Parks refused to give up her bus seat to a white man. Her action led to the Montgomery bus boycott, and eventually to the end of segregation in the South.

**AK** The U.S. bought Alaska from Russia in 1867 for $7.2 million.

5 **AZ** The Grand Canyon is up to a mile deep and over 200 miles long.

**AR** Diamonds.

6 **CA** In 1913, the temperature reached 134°F.

**CO** Tyrannosaurus Rex.

7 **CT** Noah Webster wrote America's first dictionary.

**DE** Nylon.

8 **FL** The Everglades.

**GA** The Appalachian Trail runs between Georgia and Maine.

9 **HI** Five vowels (A, E, I, O, U) and seven consonants (H, K, L, M, N, P, W) for a total of twelve letters.

**ID** Whitewater is caused by water rushing quickly over underwater obstacles, usually rocks.

10 **IL** One hundred and ten stories.

**IN** "Hoosier" is a nickname for a person from Indiana.

11 **IA** *American Gothic* was painted by Iowa artist Grant Wood.

**KS** Cowboys used to drive large herds of cattle from Texas to the railroad in Kansas.

12 **KY** The $6 billion worth of gold belongs to the U.S. government.

**LA** A *delta* is a silt deposit at the mouth of a river. *Gumbo* is a stew made with okra. A *Cajun* is a person of French ancestry.

13 **ME** West Quoddy Head residents are the farthest east.

**MD** The United States national anthem, *The Star-Spangled Banner*, was written by Maryland native Francis Scott Key.

14 **MA** The Mayflower.

**MI** The Mitten.

15 **MN** Paul Bunyan, the giant hero of many tall tales.

**MS** Mississippi is the world's leading producer of pond-raised catfish.

16 **MO** For sixteen months, from April 1860–October 1861.

**MT** A glacier is a huge sheet of ice and compacted snow.

page 17 **NE** Arbor Day.

**NV** The average rainfall is about 7 inches a year.

18 **NH** Roofs are put on bridges to save the wood from rotting.

**NJ** Thomas Edison.

19 **NM** Adobe bricks are made of clay and straw, then dried in the sun.

**NY** France gave the Statue of Liberty to the U.S. in 1886.

20 **NC** The Wright brothers: Orville flew the airplane while Wilbur ran alongside.

**ND** A Settler who was given free land (a homestead) if he farmed it.

21 **OH** Seven.

**OK** The government gave out free land in Oklahoma in 1889. Settlers who claimed land too early were called "sooners."

22 **OR** Crater Lake, about 1,900 feet deep, is the deepest lake in the United States.

**PA** Benjamin Franklin.

23 **RI** Most of Rhode Island is part of the mainland, though there are several small islands that are part of the state.

**SC** At Fort Sumter, near Charleston.

24 **SD** Laura Ingalls Wilder wrote *Little House on the Prairie* and other books about her pioneer life.

**TN** Elvis Presley, who named his mansion Graceland.

25 **TX** Texas volunteers fought a battle against Mexico in 1836, and were trapped in the Alamo.

**UT** When a swarm of crickets started eating the settlers' crops, a flock of gulls ate the insects.

26 **VT** Sap is drained from maple trees, then boiled into syrup.

**VA** Eight presidents were born there, including Washington.

27 **WA** Mount St. Helens.

**WV** Coal is made of fossilized plants that grew millions of years ago. It is burned for fuel or made into chemicals.

28 **WI** Dairy products such as milk and cheese.

**WY** Yellowstone became the world's first national park in 1872.

29 **DC** Maryland.

**Terr.** They are U.S. citizens, but can't vote in presidential elections.